MINUS 38

A STORY OF RESILIENCE

SHELLINE KOVACS

Minus 38
Copyright © 2021 by Shelline Kovacs

Tellwell Talent
www.tellwell.ca

ISBN
978-0-2288-5504-0 (Paperback)
978-0-2288-5505-7 (eBook)

DEDICATION
TO MY FAMILY

xoxo

IN MEMORY
Dad and Dwayne

"The deeper that sorrow carves into your
being, the more joy you can contain."
On Joy and Sorrow in *The Prophet* by Kahlil Gibran

SPECIAL THANKS
"THE SWEET ASSISTANT"
for your encouragement!
and
IT Support - Chris

PROCEEDS
10% of every book sold will be donated to the Centre for
Addiction and Mental Health Foundation (CAMH)

TABLE OF CONTENTS

PROLOGUE

It was a snowy mid-December evening in 1972. White, flaky snow piled up along our living room window. Dad placed his hand along the bottom of the back door and felt a cold draft making its way inside. The temperature outside was dropping, so Dad quickly turned up the baseboard heaters and placed a few rolled up towels along the bottom of door to prevent the cold air from blowing through. Mom was in the kitchen scrubbing the supper dishes. It was Dad's night to attend a support group meeting, and he asked—well, begged—Mom to come with him. She was not interested in going. I overheard Dad pleading with her to go with him that night, but she was unwilling.

My sister Jan and I shared a larger bedroom, so my siblings and I often gathered there to play our favourite board games on the floor, and tonight was no exception. We loved Kerplunk, a game where a long plastic tube with plastic straws was inserted into a tube and then dozens of marbles were thrown into the top of the tube. The object of the game was to take turns pulling out straws and dropping the fewest marbles in your section of the tray to win. In another game called Operation, we took turns mastering the skill of removing white plastic bones and organs with tweezers to win big "money." We had to be careful not to touch the metal edges as you would hear a loud buzz and Sam's (the electrified patient) nose would light up cherry red, ending your turn. The wishbone on the left side of Sam's chest looked like a chicken bone (furcular forked) and was worth a high amount of cash, so it was challenging to remove. Funny, whenever we had chicken for dinner, we would save our wishbone and let it dry out and make wishes while breaking it in half. To have your wish granted, you had to end up with the longer side of the wishbone bone in this tug of war. The plastic "broken heart" with an imprinted crack through it was on the right side of Sam's chest and not so hard to pull out as I think back. Etch a Sketch was popular back then too. It was roughly an eight- by eleven-inch red square with a gray screen and two white dials that you would turn back and forth to create drawings. To start a new drawing, you simply shook the square to clear the screen. I spent a lot of time on Etch a Sketch as I enjoyed drawing.

That evening, Dad came into our bedroom and watched us play our various games. He asked us casually what we would like to be when we grow up. I remember Jan saying a go-go dancer, and Dad laughed. I had a typewriter, so I may have said a secretary. I do not recall what Dwayne and Ben (my brothers) said, but I think one of them wanted to be a truck driver. We finished our games and started to get ready for bed. Dad said goodnight to us all as he was leaving for his meeting. Mom continued to busy herself in the kitchen doing supper dishes. I followed Dad to the front door and saw him look at Mom with disappointment as he got his long black overcoat on and laced up his black shoes. He always wore rubber covers over his shoes to protect them against wet weather. I followed him out and down the stairs as he headed to the underground garage, begging to come with him. He stopped at the staircase and quietly said "No," not in an unkind way, but with enough inflection that I knew he was serious. "Go upstairs and take care of your brothers and sister," he said. Reluctantly, I went back upstairs feeling disappointed that I was unable to go with him. I went straight to bed, as school was the next morning.

Dad never returned home from that meeting. Mom filed a missing person report with the police at the end of that week.

Christmas arrived and we had no idea where Dad could be. Mom was so distraught that she was unable to cook Christmas dinner; she just laid on the couch in a cloud of sadness and worry. I wondered if she felt guilty that she did not go with Dad that evening. We made peanut butter and jam sandwiches and had some chocolate milk. Christmas of 1972 was mostly a blur.

We went to afternoon mass on New Year's Day. Mom shared her worries with a lady that was a regular church goer before mass started. Afterwards, we were invited to supper at her place. Mom called a cab later that day, and we taxied over to the kind lady's place. The conversation at the table was around the whereabouts of my dad. We wondered why he had not called us. We all were feeling anxious and worried as we passed the food around the table. The mashed potatoes were fluffy white like the snow piled up outside the kind lady's home. Smothering them in the hot, thick gravy was comforting to us all. Dwayne asked for pepper and heavily sprinkled his food to taste. It was so nice to have a home-cooked meal, and we emptied our plates and went back for a bit more. Ben, Jan, and Dwayne grabbed some Chips Ahoy cookies and headed to the living room to watch some TV, but I decided to have tea and cookies with the adults. I felt way beyond my age of nine as I sipped my tea from a rose-patterned cup. We were in deep thought around the table, and all prayed we would hear some encouraging news soon. After a few hours we were given a lift home and invited back anytime.

Days passed, and it was time for us to return to school. I loved school and always tried to do the best I could. I aced the spelling test that week. It was usually during French when I would lose my focus and think about Mom. Each day, I wondered if she would have some new information when we got home. As each day passed with no news, I realized it was probably not going to be good. I burned a lot of energy at recess time, as I loved to run around the playground and make snow angels. When school was out each day, Dwayne and Ben played hockey until supper, slamming the puck against the concrete wall. The sound was loud and sharp. I occupied myself with Paint by Number projects, and Jan kept busy creating different hairstyles on her mannequin. Mom spent hours talking on the phone to her sister.

After school on January 11, 1973, we arrived home to the news that Dad's car had been found parked behind the Continental Can Company near the waterfront. His wallet and overcoat were found in the front seat.

We were all numb.

CHAPTER 1
Beginnings

Mom and Dad met at a dance hall in Toronto, Ontario, in the spring of 1962. Mom said that a very handsome man with blue eyes approached her for a dance and *BOOM* their romance began. They both enjoyed country music and waltzing. Their courtship was short! Mom was pregnant and expecting a baby (me) in May 1963, so wedding plans were hastily organized.

Mom was the youngest of twelve children and grew up in Douro Township/Peterborough, Ontario, along the Trent-Severn Waterway. Her mother was forty-eight years old when she had my mom. Mom often referred to herself as a "change of life" baby. Mom's parents were born in the 1890s and were turkey farmers. Her mother would bake pies for the local seniors' residence, and her dad sold canoes in the area. At sixteen years of age and with a grade eight education, Mom moved to Toronto to find a job. She worked in factories and eventually found room and board in Mimico. While at home in the kitchen, mom could peel potatoes with her eyes closed, paring knife in hand; never mind a potato peeler!

Dad was fifth in line of fourteen children and was raised in Miminegash, Prince Edward Island. The beach was just minutes behind Dad's house. Red soil and twenty-foot-high sandstone cliffs bordered the area. Fishing boats and lobster traps were a way of life on the island. Dad's parents were potato farmers. After Dad completed high school, he left the island in his early twenties and headed to Toronto to find work. He drove a taxi until he secured work with Canadian Building Materials where he drove a big cement mixer and poured concrete at different jobs all over the city of Toronto.

My parents married in November of 1962. It was a Catholic Church wedding with a traditional wedding party. Mom wore a beautiful white embroidered gown, and Dad was dressed in a black and white tailored suit. I occasionally bring out their black and white wedding photos to ponder over. They looked so happy. Mom always said her black purse ruined the wedding photo, however, that purse represented a forewarning of events yet to unfold.

My parents had four children: me in 1963, Dwayne (1964), Janice (1965) and Ben (1967). Mom stayed home and Dad went to work. It was like we lived in *Leave It to Beaver.* Dad would come home each night to a big pot of mashed potatoes. "Bud the Spud," a Stompin' Tom Connors song, could have been played around our kitchen table each night. "It's Bud the spud from the bright red mud rolling down the highway smiling…." Dad would eat a mountain of PEI mashed potatoes smothered in butter and sprinkled with salt and pepper! Mom always served Dad dinner and then got us bathed and ready for bed.

In the summer of 1969, my parents put together a swing set and slide in our backyard. Ben was toddling around by then, and I would push him in the swing. We had several gooseberry bushes and a large pear tree. I remember picking the gooseberries and enjoying the tangy, juicy flavour. Mom and Dad would pick pears off the tree for us to snack on.

Every Saturday night we watched *Hockey Night in Canada* while drinking pop and eating potato chips. Dad would enjoy his stubby-bottled Red Cap beer and cheer for the Canadiens against the Toronto Maple Leafs. On Sundays we went to morning mass and returned home for a family lunch. We spent sunny afternoons playing in our backyard and rainy ones in the basement. A special treat before bed on Sunday was watching *Walt Disney Presents*.

Mom spent a lot of time in the kitchen puttering around with different tasks. Dad set up an ironing board in the kitchen as Mom ironed everything. Each kitchen cupboard was decorated with a star that was removed from the Seagram's Five Star Whisky bottle. Oddly, Mom would stick them on the cupboards for decoration.

November 1962 Wedding

The Four Children

Dad often wrote letters to his family back in Prince Edward Island. I admired the flow and gracefulness of his penmanship. He wrote with his left hand as I do. I paid close attention to his writing as it predicted my special interest in understanding why people write the way they do. Later in life I became very interested in studying handwriting and analyzing it. I was fortunate enough to have been able to retrieve some writing from both parents, so I did a short analysis of their writing to help me get to know them better.

Dad's writing sample reveals a slant that is moderate to high responsiveness. Feelings would be shown easily. A light to moderate pressure on the pen indicates past intense emotional experiences would fade over time. Well rounded *e* circles indicate broad-mindedness. His looped *t* and *d* show sensitiveness to criticism. Secretiveness demonstrated in the letter *o*. The most evident trait in the sample was his persistence, which is noted by his tied stroke in the letter H revealing a spirit of not giving up so easy.

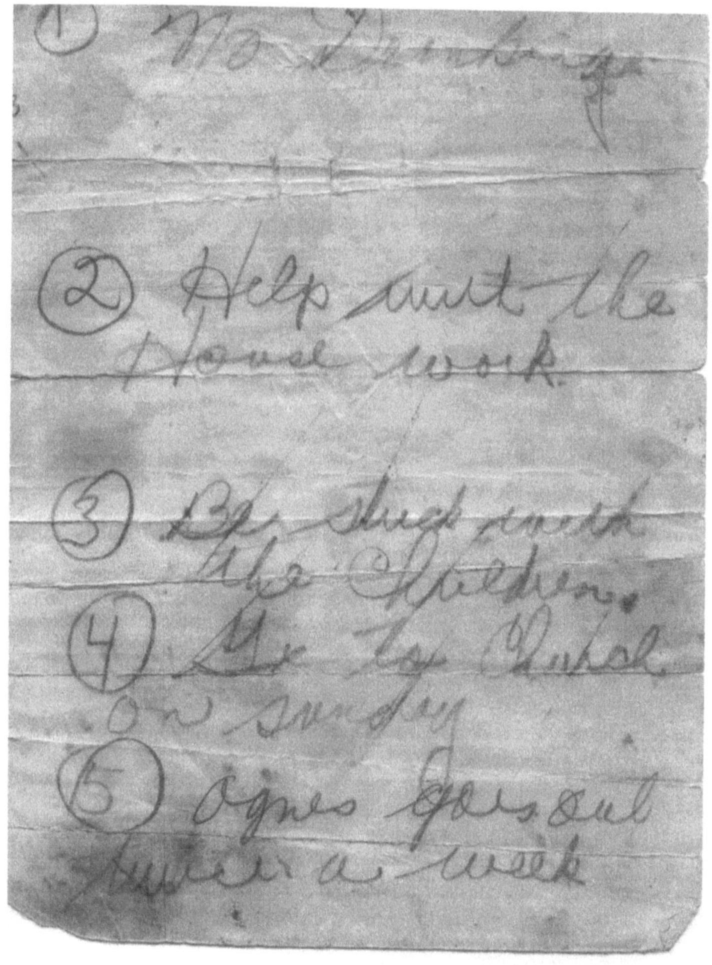

Dad's Writing Sample 1

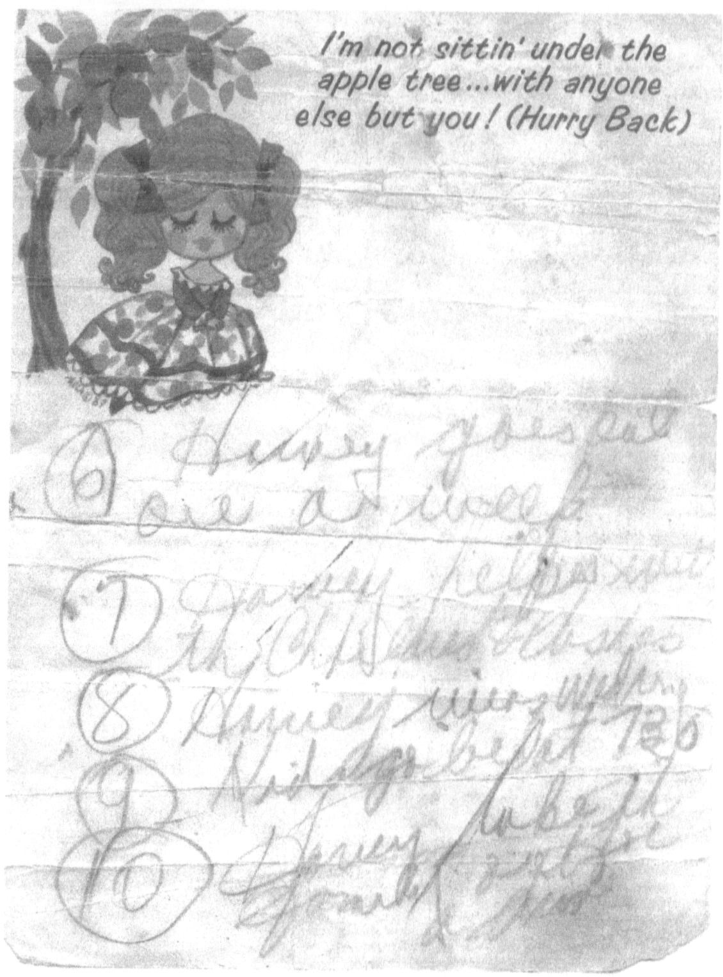

Dad's Writing Sample 2

Mom's writing samples reveal a slant indicating a mild to moderate emotional response to situations. Occasional withdrawal (self-interest) is also apparent. She applied moderate to deep pressure on the pen which reveals a deep emotional nature. She felt past experiences just like the day they happened. Mom's repression (denying thoughts and feelings to a point of being driven to unconscious mind and no longer aware of their influence) in her handwriting is clear as there are many pinched and retraced letters. Her flat-topped *r* indicates manual dexterity, which was evident when sewing something quickly or using a paring knife.

Mom's Writing Samples

CHAPTER 2

Earliest Memories

My earliest memory of my dad is a flashback to a beautiful summer day in 1969. We lived in a rented three-bedroom home in the St. Clair Avenue West and Christie area, now called Bracondale Hill in Toronto, Ontario. Dad's brother Tom happened to be in Toronto that summer to visit family, so he swung by our house that day to pick up Dad and I to go visit Uncle Pete. We excitedly jumped into the convertible! I sat on Dad's lap—seatbelts were not yet mandatory—and off we went. The beautiful notes of "My Cherie Amour" by Stevie Wonder spilled out from the radio and serenaded the streets…la, la, la, la, la, la…as we sped along. Although the song seems to relate to a special lady a man believes is beyond reach, it spoke to me in a different way. It was about a father and daughter spending some special time together. "Lovely as a summer day, pretty little one that I adore," are special memories I carry. Every time I hear the song, that special day flows back to me. "Maybe someday, you'll see my face among the crowd. Maybe someday, I'll share your little distant cloud" tells my story.

Work boots caked with cement was a vision I recall at our front door so long ago. Dad drove a concrete mixer for a living. He would transport mixed concrete to the construction sites and pour concrete for a living. I remember him stopping by on his lunch hour in his truck so we could all have a turn sitting with him in the driver's seat. The CN Tower would have been his next project had he not disappeared. Dad worked hard for his money to support his young family, as most loving fathers do.

I knew the days Dad was tired or upset about something because he would rest on the couch with his body turned inward and his long right leg stretched over top of the couch. When he was happy, he would step dance east coast style, and I would laugh and try to follow along. He enjoyed playing hockey with his company team and liked to bowl. I treasured the session of learning how to draw a three-dimensional square with Dad. He would not let me go until I learned it.

Dad drove a 1967 Country Squire station wagon, a popular model for families compared to the caravans that came much later, with a red leather interior. There were rumble seats at the very back of the vehicle, and it felt like a roller coaster ride when we zipped along the winding, steep hill on the north side of Davenport Road. I have visions of me ducking to the floor and holding on to the back of the front seats for dear life! We moved freely inside the vehicle, sometimes sitting in the rumble seats, and sometimes moving up to sit behind Dad with our chin resting on the top of the leather seat. Dad would often look in his rear-view mirror and flash a big smile or a quick wink for me. I felt we were liked-minded spirits!

Family vacations meant driving down east to see Dad's family in Prince Edward Island. Our Squire's rumble seats folded down and gave us a place to sleep, and we brought pillows and blankets to make it comfortable. Dad drove all night with little rest. I would periodically awaken and rest my head on the seat behind him, watching him drive. Again, he would smile and wink! We took the ferry across to the island. It was exciting to board the ramp and see all the other vehicles climbing on to the ferry. Once we were parked, we would all go up to the top deck to see miles of the North Cumberland Strait and breathe in the fresh, briny Atlantic air. We eagerly watched for the deep red soil that made Prince Edward Island so captivating.

I have a few memories of the house Dad grew up in. It was a two-story white home with black trimmed windows on acres of farmland. Upon entry we were in the kitchen, and off to the left was a door that led to the hay loft where Dad and his brothers slept as children. To the right of the kitchen was entry into the living room. Stairs lead up to my grandparents' bedroom and washroom. An old barn that housed three black horses and lots of hay was located a little distance from the house. I do not remember the horses' names, but they were big with shiny black coats.

Gramma served molasses and fresh bread each morning for breakfast. One day she boiled some lobster in a deep pot, and I can still remember the screeching sounds of the poor lobsters being boiled alive! My brothers, sister and I always collected blueberries from the bush at the back of the house and enjoyed them for an afternoon snack. The Gulf of St. Lawrence was Dad's back yard, and I remember a long stretch of red sandy beach and the smell of Irish moss, an edible red seaweed which was traditionally harvested by many islanders. When boiled, it yields a jelly that is used as a thickening agent and in medicine. We were down on the beach swimming one day, and I was greeted with mouthful of saltwater. I discovered you could float on the water much easier because of the salt that made the water denser. The ocean represented freedom to me as it seemed one could go anywhere one wanted. What lay at the bottom of the ocean was a mystery in the making.

Wasps swarmed around the front door of my grandparents' house one morning during our last vacation with Dad. We had to quickly run out the door and run as fast as we could to avoid getting stung. The wasp's nest was sprayed, and the nest destroyed after a few days.

Between swimming, picking berries and walking barefoot along the country road to buy candy and ice cream, my brothers, sister, and I loved our connection to our father's birthplace.

CHAPTER 3

The Ford Hotel
(1971-72)

I have a vivid memory of hearing my mom calling a taxi to come as fast as possible to pick us up. She would tell us to quickly change out of our pajamas because we had to leave immediately. Sometimes we just left in our pajamas. It was alarming and disruptive! Dwayne was often car sick, so we had to pull over to the side of the road in the middle of the night so he could vomit. Each time Dad was not home at the regular supper hour, Mom would suspect he was at the tavern, and she did not want to be home when he got back. Mom was nervous around people who drank too much. The Horseshoe Tavern showcased Stompin' Tom Connors' band. "You'll have found the stompin' grounds of all my friends and me," they sang. Dad was hanging out there more often as my parents were not getting along. On those nights we raced through the dark Toronto streets in a cab to Mom's "stompin' grounds," The Ford Hotel.

The Ford Hotel was built in 1928 at Dundas Street, east of Bay Street in downtown Toronto. It was designed with three adjoining towers that were twelve stories high with the main lobby as the base of the hotel. The bus terminal was located across the road, so many travellers arrived in Toronto and stayed in the hotel, while others were families immigrating to Canada who temporarily lived there. Nightly theatre and musical entertainment were offered in the lounge. The performers often stayed as guests, and it was exciting to stay in the same place as these people. One entertainer of note was Dizzy Gillespie, a famous trumpeter that shaped the sounds of modern jazz.

Upon entering the hotel, I often heard a piano or trumpet mixing with the sounds of glasses clinking as they were bussed down a hallway. Crowds of people in the main lobby carrying luggage would pile into the manually operated elevator. It was always jam-packed, and if people could not get on, they seemed disappointed and annoyed as they glanced at their wristwatches. A man dressed in a uniform with gold tassels hanging from his sleeves would slide the brass metal gates across. The stiff clank of metal echoed in the air as we were locked in the elevator like prisoners being locked up in jail. People would shout out what floor they wanted, and the operator would oblige by pressing numerous buttons. Each time we stopped at a floor, it seemed to be a big ordeal as we waited for the floor to align to the elevator. It took a long time to get to each floor. Were these other people running away like we were?

Our room always had two large queen beds, a desk with a bright light and a Bible in the bedside drawer. Sometimes when I was unable to sleep, I would flip the pages of the Bible and wonder why it was there. Other times I would look out the window down to the streetlights and watch the cars go by and the people scurry about. The curtains were a dark, heavy velvet that blocked out whatever it was Mom was so afraid of. It felt strange to wake up in a hotel room. I missed my own bed and the familiarity of the possessions I had in my room.

Sometimes I would hear people in the hallways, and Mom would tell us to be very quiet so she could listen. She always made our situation seem bigger than it was, but she clearly did not want to be home when Dad decided to come back. I wondered if he would call and let her know he was going out after work or not even bother. Coming home to an empty house would have been lonely and upsetting for Dad.

One morning we taxied home early after a night at the Ford and saw that Dad's car was still parked outside our house. Mom anxiously knocked on a neighbour's door and asked if we could come in and wait until Dad left for work. A Japanese family brought us into their serene home and served us tea and juice while Mom peered through their fancy sheer curtains in the front room. Once Dad's car was gone, we returned home.

On another Ford visit, Mom took us to a park for an afternoon where she met a lady named Mrs. Caney, who was sitting with her two daughters, Katie and Sarah, on a park bench. They befriended each other and seemed to share the same problems. Mrs. Caney was a recently divorced woman who seemed angry and complained a lot. After a few hours of playing in the park, Mom and Mrs. Caney agreed that we were all going to the Ford for the night. Off we went in two taxi cabs with all of us feeling confused. The night was crazy, we did not get much sleep. We all stayed in one room and had to share the two queen beds; some of us slept on the floor. Mrs. Caney's oldest daughter was screaming and crying as she wanted to leave. She did not like the room and fought all night with her sister over the sleeping arrangements. We all left the next morning and never returned to the hotel. The Ford Hotel closed for good in 1973 after several tragedies took place.

Mom and Mrs. Caney continued their friendship, and I had regular visits to see Katie and Sarah at their apartment. I was nine years old, and Katie was eleven, so I enjoyed hanging out with an older friend. Each time we visited, Katie and I would play the 1972 top of the chart hit "American Pie" by Don McLean on her record player. How that music used to make *US* smile. We would dance and sing our little hearts out… "And I knew if I had my chance, that I could make those people dance, and maybe they'd be happy for a while…" All the kids were up dancing, but we could not get Mom or Mrs. Caney to dance. Instead, we were told to turn the music down. Katie, being her deviant self, ignored her mother's request but eventually turned it down.

Sometimes we would flee to a church basement not far from our house. The sleeping arrangements were rows of cots set up with gray blankets on them. I would hear children crying and people shuffling around throughout the night. The next morning, we were served a communal breakfast of terrible porridge, cold toast, and apple juice. The women and children looked distressed like us. I wanted to go home so badly and was tired of this running around. Dad did not mistreat us in any way, and I can only speak of one time that he brought home five or six buddies from the tavern who slept on our living room floor. There was no commotion other than sounds of men snoring. They were gone very early before breakfast. I imagine it would have been a Friday or

Saturday, and no doubt because Dad was so hospitable. Mom was furious! My parents were mismatched.

Sometimes Mom would arrange for us to stay at her Aunt Lorrie's (her sister) or Aunt Wendy's (her sister-in-law) place. After Dwayne's inevitable car sickness, we would finally arrive at the door, the night lights would come on and the door would open. It was tight quarters at Aunt Lorrie's, and she seemed annoyed and thought Mom exaggerated all this commotion, but she always made room for us. Other times we stayed at Aunt Wendy's (her sister-in-law) who was divorced and seemed a little more tolerant of us staying the night.

I can only think that these flights from home in the middle of the night were triggered by Mom's childhood memories. She told me her brother was involved in a bar brawl that resulted in him being charged with manslaughter. This was devastating news for Mom's parents, and it was a family disgrace as alcohol was never permitted in their home. Mom also said she had returned home past curfew from a date one night and tiptoed quietly upstairs to her room. Her father was a very strict man who did not hesitate to pour a cold bucket of water over her if she did not get up early to attend to her chores. Mom woke up after a terrifying nightmare that night and discovered she had jumped right through her partially open single-paned bedroom window. She had fallen about twelve feet and cut her stomach open badly on some glass. Her mother poured flour into her wound to slow the bleeding while they waited for the ambulance. Once Mom arrived at the hospital, she needed several pints of blood as she had lost way too much. These two incidents impacted her significantly, and they made me wonder what other experiences she may have undergone in her young life.

On a lighter note, Aunt Lorrie told me a childhood story about her and Mom picking a basket of berries in the field by their home. Their mother enticed the girls by offering to bake a pie for the first one to come back with their basket full. Mom filled half her basket with berries and the rest was filled with leaves. To add some appeal, she threw some berries on top of the leaves to make the basket look full. Mom hurried back to the house and got the pie that day! It reminds me of the fairy tale *The Tortoise and the Hare*. However, it was not slow and steady that won the race this time; Aunt Lorrie called it favouritism. Aunt Lorrie and Mom were close but had plenty of sibling rivalry between them. It would have been great to hear more stories of Mom's childhood, but Mom was usually reticent when I asked questions about her upbringing.

Eventually, my parents parted. Mom had found an upper floor of a house very close to the Exhibition Place for us to rent. The landlord lived on the main floor and had a big German shepherd. We had quite a flight of stairs to climb, but once upstairs it was a bright and clean apartment with of lots of windows. We started at a new school that fall and made new friends. Dad found a rooming house to board at nearby. He made regular visits and tried to make amends with Mom. One evening from my bedroom, I heard my parents discussing new rules that had to be followed for their relationship to work. Dad had to help with chores and be stricter with us. There would be designated nights out for both and church on Sundays. Lastly, there would be no drinking allowed! I heard Dad leave that night and watched him walk down the street through my bedroom window until I could not see him anymore. Resting with my head on my pillow I prayed that things would get better.

One afternoon Dad arrived with a wonderful surprise: a little puppy—we were so excited! As the weeks went on my mother found the puppy too hard to care for, and she gave the pup away one day when we were at school. She broke the news to us during our lunch break, and we all wept. We were inconsolable, and our sadness turned to anger. Chocolate milk went flying all over the table. We did not return to school that afternoon. I can just imagine how upset Dad would have been.

Upon entering through the front door one day when we came home from school, the German shepherd darted towards us and jumped on Dwayne. Luckily, he turned to the corner wall quickly enough and covered his face. The dog set upon him and clawed the back of his head so much that he required stitches. The sound of us entering the house always alerted the shepherd, as they are inherently guard dogs, but he was usually leashed, or their living room door was closed. Not that day. Dad met Mom and Dwayne at the hospital, and they returned home hours later. Dwayne went straight to bed, and Dad returned to his place.

The dog was the catalyst for us moving again, and we ended up in the suburbs away from Toronto. For grade four, I started at yet another new school. I always found it awkward because I was having to make new friends all over again. Walking around alone at recess I spotted the cliquey groups and wondered who my friends would be. It sure did not take long to join in on a game of tag and make new friends. Dad continued to visit but had a little more distance to travel as he worked in Toronto. Mom and Dad would sometimes go for drives to have some time alone, and a neighbourhood teenager would come over to care for us. It was just fifty cents an hour back then for babysitting and a quarter more after midnight.

The day Dad lost his job was the hardest. I do not know all the details, but what I understood was he was caught drinking on his lunch hour and fired on the spot. It is not unusual for people to have a drink on their lunch hour. I wondered how much he had consumed and if he deserved to be fired, but the details of what transpired that day were not available to me. In today's world, companies may have suspended him or given him a warning. Employee assistance programs are also in place these days. Dad's employment record of sixteen years with Canadian Building Materials was impeccable despite that day. He was the sole provider for our family, and I think he was harshly reprimanded!

Dad moved back in with us and quickly found work. He would come home each evening wearing a solid blue uniform, and he looked exhausted. One evening he punched numbers into a calculator at the kitchen table as I passed him yellow cards one by one. Then he would stack them in a neat pile. I am not sure, but I think the cards were records of his productivity that day. I wish I knew the company name and what his job was; I am guessing he could have been a driver. Strangely, Mom mentioned that when she contacted the company, they claimed he never worked for them. I wonder if she was confused or just oblivious about who he worked for during that time. I suspect it was a temp agency like Manpower. Weeks turned into a few months, and Dad was struggling with his new job and a failing marriage. On the days he was home he would drive us to school. Dad appeared very gloomy.

CHAPTER 4

Deliberate-Accident

On January 19, 1973, my teacher asked me to meet Dwayne at the school office. We waited for our younger brother and sister to arrive, and then were instructed to go straight home. The snow was falling heavily, and I turned around a few times to see the long trail of our footprints as we nervously marched home. We were going to hear some news about Dad. Many thoughts ran through our heads. We were all silent and scared. I thought maybe he was found injured and everything would be okay. Was he going to explain where he was and tell us about his new place? Mom and Dad could not live together anymore. I prayed he was not dead. The tension mounting on our walk home always reminds me of the movie *Jaws*. When the killer shark gets close to attacking and devouring its prey, the music rises and a creepy, frantic feeling sinks to the bottom of my stomach.

We arrived home and all walked up the same staircase where I had begged Dad to let me go with him that night. A white-collared priest was sitting in our orange chair by the sliding glass door. Mom had been sobbing and sat still. We all sat down, and we were told that the angels decided to take our father to heaven to care for and protect him. No one immediately explained how he died as the emphasis was more on him leaving us to be with God. Our heads dropped to the floor, and I remember staring at the green shag carpet for a very long time. We were all devastated!

Earlier that day, the police knocked on the door carrying a bag of my dad's clothing and informed my mother that his body was recovered by a harbour patrol officer. He was floating about five feet off the wall behind Continental Can Company not far from where his car was found days earlier. The coroner's report indicated it was a "Suffocate Drowning." There were no traces of alcohol or drugs in my dad's body. The coroner's report said he was found about eight days after his death and speculated that January 11, 1973, was the day the tragedy occurred. His body was slightly decomposed and there was no evidence of trauma. The coroner wrote that his personal history indicated he had lost his job and was dealing with depression. Mom said Dad was found on Cherry Beach. In a warped way, was she sparing us the real details? She said that the battery of his car was missing and that she was not sure if he slipped or decided to end his life. She mentioned there was no alcohol or drugs in his body.

There were mixed stories and speculation of what exactly happened, and rumours started floating around our neighbourhood. It was cold—it was January—why would Dad have been found like that? Mom sometimes wondered if he slipped on the ice and fell into the water. This may be the case, but it was a reckless and unusual decision to wander down around the water that time of the year. Other times she mentioned that "It was a good thing I didn't go that night, as I may not be here today." Her last thought came from a psychic reading where she was told there was a very tall lady with glasses dressed in a long trench coat smoking a long-tipped cigarette, and a middle-aged man with a moustache very near at the time of my father's death. Mom was hinting that maybe Dad owed money and that foul play was involved. So many theories and never any firm conclusion.

Mom sold Dad's car to a gentleman that lived in the building adjacent to ours, which seemed thoughtless. We did not need that memory flashing in our face every day. One mild snowy day, I remember playing Red Rover, Red Rover in the front of our apartment building when I saw our station wagon pass by. I looked over and wished it were Dad driving his car again. I ran across the grass with so much vengeance when I was called over that I easily busted my way through the arms of friends. Sometimes we would build snow forts and have snowball fights. Playing outdoors for hours was not unusual as it was a simpler time before the days of internet and video games. When the temperatures really plummeted, we would stay inside and play our board games or watch TV shows such as *The Partridge Family*, *The Brady Bunch* or *Family Affair* that incidentally portrayed families who had experienced parental loss. I found comfort and enlightenment in these shows, as they reminded me that other families also dealt with grief at such an early age.

The rest of the time before the funeral was fuzzy, much like the TV going staticky for a period.

CHAPTER 5

Funeral 1

The funeral home was in downtown Toronto. It was a rainy, grey, and slushy late morning. Mom, wearing a plain black dress with black buttons on the sleeves, led us into the funeral home. We were greeted by a man in a black suit who directed us to a room filled with lots of people and many colourful flowers where Dad was resting. I sat up front with my mom and my aunts while my siblings sat a little farther back with an uncle. I cried out loud intermittently. My Aunt Terra put me on her lap during the funeral visitation and began complaining about runs in her pantyhose. She was trying hard to console me with her nervous, inappropriate laughter. I glanced over at Dad; he looked different. His face appeared "sunken." He was wearing a purple dress shirt and black pants. Guilt, sadness, anger, regret, and numbness were plastered all over the faces of those in attendance.

I was told my father's boss from Canada Building Materials was in the room. Apparently, he felt some accountability for what had happened along with major regrets that he had fired Dad. My grandpa (Dad's father) flew in from Prince

Edward Island and sat silently in the room. One of Dad's brothers, Uncle Ryan, was so distraught that he reached into the coffin and shouted, "Wake up, wake up!!" He was quickly pulled back and taken out of the room. At that point, my Uncle Lawrence took me out of the funeral home, and we walked the streets for a block or two and then returned. It was pouring rain as we walked quietly under a big black umbrella.

The final goodbye was a few days later at the church we frequented. The church was decorated with brightly coloured stained-glass windows. Inside, I remember many wooden bench-pews and lots of Bibles. A second-tier balcony was available at the back of the church for extra seating. We were up early, and I was trying to decide on whether I wanted to go. I was wavering and feeling to upset. I knew my classmates and teacher would be attending. I finally told Mom I did not want to go, and she was fine with my decision. My siblings attended, but I do not remember who stayed back with me that morning. Mom put down newspaper print all over her bedroom floor along with all my paints, brushes and my latest project that had a black velvet background. I just wanted to paint and be left alone.

About a week after Dad's funeral, I was painting on the floor in Mom's room when a "paranormal" experience occurred that I will never forget. As I looked over at Mom's dresser, Dad's face suddenly appeared in the mirror. It was very pale with no expression, and he did not say anything. Then it quickly disappeared. I did not run but just sat still and waited to see if it would appear again, but it never did. My face turned "a whiter shade of pale," and it reminds me of Procol Harum's words: "The room was humming harder as the ceiling flew away...." It was Dad's final goodbye! I kept that whole experience to myself as I did not feel anyone would believe me. But it truly happened.

Dad at Greenwood Racetrack 1968

CHAPTER 6

Life after Dad

It was close to Valentine's Day, and we kids were at the kitchen table addressing our Valentine's cards to give to our friends at school. My friend next door was going to deliver our cards, as we were not returning to school yet. Suddenly, there was a knock at the door, so I went to answer it. It was the gentleman that we sold our car to. He was wearing a blue lumber jacket and had long hair tied back in a ponytail. He smiled, said hello, and wanted to talk to my mom. He carried a brown envelope in his hand. Mom quickly came to the door, and he passed her an envelope he had found buried under the rumble seats of his vehicle that used to be ours. He decided not to open it, as it was sealed. He expressed condolences and left swiftly. Mom opened it and found a few one-hundred-dollar bills and a piece of note paper that listed the rules Mom wanted for the marriage to work. I asked if I could keep the note, and Mom passed it to me quietly. The list went into my memory box, as I remember the night of them discussing the rules Mom had requested. Quietly, I thought about what Dad's requests should have been for the list. It appeared he was saving money, and I wondered if he won at the Greenwood Racetrack. Mom sat in the living room for a long time after putting the envelope in her bedroom.

We were off school for a long while; it felt like a month or two. My best friend at the time came by to visit and brought me some clothes she was no longer wearing. Ironically, her father had passed away a few years prior, so we found comfort in each other. The previous summer and fall we had spent a great deal of our time together riding our bikes around the neighbourhood and stopping for an ice cream sandwich or whatever treat we fancied. We were good buddies, and Mom recognized that she was important to me now. Occasionally, Mom gave me permission to have a sleepover at her home. We often made popcorn and chatted about our latest crush while listening to the 1973 "Sound Explosion" album. One night while laying on our pillows, we wondered what heaven looked liked. I pictured it to be very colourful with a never-ending supply of Jujubes and Smarties. My friend added that no dentist would be needed as nobody would get cavities. Everybody up there had their own fluffy white cloud to rest on. Blankets were not necessary as the temperature was always warm. Everyone in heaven sparkled with joy and peace; no one was ever sad. We thought about the idea of a huge television screen that people up in heaven could tune in to so they could check on us down here on Earth.

Reflecting on this time, I found the movie *My Girl* (1991) had a strong connection to my life. Ten-year-old Vada was consumed by the loss of her mother who died of complications after childbirth. Vada blamed herself and thought she killed her mother. Vada sometimes plugged her ears with her fingers and frantically sang "Doo Wah Diddy Diddy" (Manfred

Mann) as a way of distracting herself from the overwhelming emotions. My way of dealing with the emotions was to run as fast as I could until I exhausted myself, much like Vada did when she distraughtly stormed out of her house after attending the unfortunate funeral viewing of her best friend Thomas J. Vada eventually confronted her father and asked if it was her fault that her mother died, and her dad explained that it was not her fault and sometimes things like this just happen. I did not blame myself but did wonder if I had been old enough to drive or was able to follow Dad that very night in a taxi—boldly disobeying his order to go back upstairs—could have prevented the outcome.

It was a beautiful spring-like day when my siblings and I returned to school. We had a long walk to get to school, and we were all excited to go back and play with our friends. I remember wearing a new spring dress that was purple, and I carried a lime green skipping rope. I was happy to be back and quickly involved myself in a skipping game called Double Dutch. "Apples, peaches, pears and plums, tell me when your birthday comes" everyone said as I jumped like a kangaroo to avoid the rope. If I had been a kangaroo at that moment, my pouch would have carried all my grief. My best friend and I started riding our bikes again. Track and field started up, and Dwayne and I would try out for many events. Getting back to school and having a regular routine was vital for our well-being.

We attended church on a regular basis after the funeral. We had no car now. My mom never drove, so we got to places by walking, taking a bus or taxi. We usually walked a good forty minutes to get to the church, and when we arrived, we always lit a white candle for Dad and sat close to the front.

After mass, we would turn around and walk another forty minutes home. We would often stop at Dunkin' Donuts so we could all pick out our favourite doughnut. Most of the time Jan and I chose the chocolate double dipped, and the honey dipped was Ben's choice. Sometimes we would sit and have our doughnut in the shop and other times enjoy it as we walked home.

One Sunday we were returning home from mass and we decided to take a short cut down a grassy hill. Mom was dressed in a cherry red polyester pant suit and new black platform shoes. She started down the hill slowly, but suddenly turned over on her ankle and fell. Dwayne and I helped her up and led her by the arms back home. It turned out she sprained her ankle badly and was on crutches for a good while. We had a Red Cross worker by the name of Mrs. Frederick come to help us while Mom's ankle healed. I felt the need to scrub the kitchen floor—scrubbing and squeezing out the mop into a pail all morning long—every day for about a week. The pail was refilled with fresh soapy water numerous times. Mom was bothered as she cried, "What is she doing? My floors are a mess!" Mrs. Frederick whispered, "She needs to do this. It is her way of dealing with things." I knew Mrs. Frederick was a smart woman at that point. Finally, after a week I stopped scrubbing the floors and knew I could not fix things or make it all better. Mom's ankle started feeling better, so Mrs. Frederick moved on to her next family in need.

We spent our first summer without Dad simply and close to home. We hung at the park with friends and enjoyed our summer treats. Mom had sporadic visits from Aunt Lorrie and neighbours offering help if needed.

Around the fall of 1973, Mom had a nervous breakdown and was hospitalized for about a month. It seemed she had been functioning on shock mode for almost nine months before she emotionally collapsed. Mrs. Frederick had moved on to another assignment, so we had a very strict German Red Cross worker come to stay with us. Her name was hard to pronounce so we just did the best we could with it. We did not accept her very well, as we found her very stern and bossy. If our dishes were not rinsed properly, she would make us repeat the rinse until she was satisfied.

Playing outside until the streetlights came on was typical for us, and if it rained, we would hang out in our bedrooms. Avoiding the German lady as much as possible was the game plan. She was nothing like Mrs. Frederick, who was a kind and relaxed lady. Mom returned home after a month, and we were happy to see her feeling better and ecstatic to see that bossy homemaker go. Mom was prescribed Valium, a popular drug many women used back then to help them cope with difficulties. It reminded me of the Rolling Stones' song, "Mother's Little Helper": "Doctor, please, some more of these…as she goes running for the shelter of her mother's little helper."

Mom purchased new bikes for us all, and we spent a lot of time riding them while listening to music like "Loco-Motion" by Little Eva: "Chug-a chug-a motion like a railroad train now (Come on baby do the locomotion) …" blasted from our neighbour's window. At the same time there was a locomotion of visitors dropping in to visit. Aunt Lorrie and Aunt Beatrice came by to see how we all were doing, as well as some ladies from the church and various neighbours.

Around this time, we made the hard visit to the cemetery and left special cards that we made at school for Dad. Mom placed flowers by his gravesite. I knelt and traced Dad's name, birthdate, and death date with my index finger. I imagined the letters in his cursive writing. My siblings stooped down to watch me. We did not stay too long and gazed quickly at other stones as we made our way out of the cemetery. Our visits ended because getting to the cemetery was a problem, so Mom sent flowers each year on Dad's birthday.

The Royal Winter Fair was running through November, and a friend invited me along with her older brother to attend. Mom let me go after she spoke to the older brother and was reassured that I would be safely brought home. Having a break from all the ruckus at home was just what I needed. We had a wonderful time, but my arrival home was much later than Mom expected. She was crying and yelling that I should have been home much earlier as she needed my help with things around the house. My friend and her brother could hear the commotion that went on behind our closed doors, and I felt so humiliated.

Christmas of 1973 was quickly approaching; it was a crippling time for my mother. She rested on the couch unable to get up. It was especially hard, as it was this time a year prior that Dad went missing. Mom gave me a few hundred dollars to go Christmas shopping at Towers Department Store, so I pushed the cart around and filled it up with gifts for my brothers and sister. I liked doing it, as I felt so grown up for just ten years old. I wrapped each gift and placed them under the tree. Mom appreciated the help and gave me some extra cash to thank me. We ordered takeout for Christmas dinner, and we were all fine with that. It was the Christmas that needed to pass.

Mercifully, the calendar flipped to 1974. Mom was having trouble with depression in January and was back in the hospital for a couple of weeks. Luckily, Mrs. Frederick returned during that time to help. We were all occupied with school, homework and seeing our friends. We felt comfortable knowing Mrs. Frederick had returned to help. Mom returned home later in January and was once again feeling better; apparently her medications had been adjusted. Mrs. Frederick decided to stay a few more days to make sure Mom was okay. We loved Mrs. Frederick; she was like a special aunt or gramma to us.

June arrived quickly, and we all passed our grades except for Janice. She was having trouble, and the teacher thought it was best to have her repeat the year. She was a later December baby so that made some sense. Mom signed us all up for a two-week overnight camping trip. I decided not to go, as I felt Mom needed me to stay back to keep her company. While my siblings were away, Mom and I would go for morning walks to the store and pick-up groceries we needed. I often prepared us sandwiches and a green salad for lunch. Later in the afternoon, Mom would boil the kettle and enjoy a hot cup of Red Rose tea and her favourite fig newton cookies. Mom collected the little porcelain figurines that came in the box of Red Rose. A collection of animals like the turtle, squirrel and hedgehog were displayed on a shelf in the living room. Some evenings she would go to bingo with a friend across the hall. She had her own collection of bingo chips that were red, blue, green, and yellow that she carried in a plastic container. Occasionally, she would come back with a win of fifty to a hundred dollars. Mom loved bingo. I would stay back with the neighbours and watch TV.

Other evenings, if Mom were in the mood, we would listen to some Don Messer reruns on TV. She also liked to play "Harper Valley P.T.A." by Jeannie C. Riley (a huge hit in 1968) on our record player. "I wanna tell you all a story 'bout a Harper Valley widow wife…." Mom regularly went to the hairdresser and liked to wear rose-coloured lipstick. Her favourite perfume was Taboo, the fragrance that came in a black long-necked bottle. She dressed fashionably in mini-skirts and halter tops that were popular during that time. "Mrs. Johnson you're wearin' your dresses way too high, it's reported you've been…goin' wild…." Mom was never part of the PTA or running wild, but she certainly gave some thought to dating again. Each week she would read the Companions section of the *Toronto Star* and circle the ads that interested her. Mom shared her approach for meeting blind dates one night at the kitchen table. Her blind date would be given a description of what she would be wearing, but Mom would show up in a totally different outfit. She figured if she did not like what she saw, she could always walk away.

We spent our last evening alone with a nice supper of pork chops, corn, and potatoes that we cooked together. Dessert was a chocolate popsicle served on a white plate. We both blissfully indulged. Once the popsicle was gone, we were quickly brought back to our reality with the anticipated arrival of my brothers and sister. It felt good to have that special time with Mom and to see that she was feeling well again.

CHAPTER 7

Water

A fear for a short while

Stand up to this bully or play hide & seek

Do I use a flashlight to really see it?

Do I wear a life jacket to stay afloat?

Or use a magic wand to zap it away?

Red rover, red rover.... here it comes; hold tight and do not let it break through!

Late at night I can wrap my old blanket around me like armour to protect me.

Sometimes my feet do not need a cover, I can let them be free...there is no Boogeyman to pull me under......

I thought a lot about water after Dad died. Water is a gift to the Earth, people, animals, and plants. It was enjoyable to watch the rain dance heavily on the pavement, filled with suspense. When we were little children, we would run and play in the rain. If thunder and lightning hit, Mom would holler for us to hurry back to our veranda for protection. We would take one last splash in the puddles as we opened our mouths wide and gulped the raindrops down.

Spinning my umbrella on the way to school and listening to the raindrops dance on the top of my umbrella was like music to my ears. B.J. Thomas' "Raindrops Keep Fallin' on My Head" was a huge hit in the 1970s and topped the Billboard charts. "The blues they send to meet me won't defeat me; it won't be long till happiness steps up to greet me." It was a song that lifted my spirits.

After the rain stopped, the worms would come out to visit and play on the streets. I would find a tiny stick or use my finger to lightly nudge the worms so they would wiggle along the sidewalk. There was always something cozy about being at home and listening to the rain. It was much like a sedative that helped calm me.

I remember Mom with her different coloured rain caps coming home with the groceries. I could often smell Juicy Fruit gum on her breath. She would walk a least thirty minutes pulling her grocery cart to get home, and if it were raining, the soaking wet paper grocery bags would be ripping apart by the time she walked in the door. Mom would hail a cab down during heavy rain storms. The groceries never lasted that long, as we emptied the fridge and cupboards as fast as Mom could fill them. Sometimes, on rainy days Mom would forget about her laundry that was hanging outside; therefore, she would wait until the sun returned to dry everything. Her preference was always to hang laundry outside as it had a fresher scent than the dryer.

Mom would rest in the evenings after all her chores were completed and enjoy her favourite soda, Fresca. The television did not interest Mom, but occasionally she would watch *I Love Lucy* and laugh a little. Aunt Lorrie would call routinely and sometimes invite us out for a swim. She had a beautiful pool surrounded by trees in her back yard, but Mom declined most times. She was not a swimmer but would dangle her feet by the water when we did visit.

Dwayne and I enjoyed swimming in the summer months. We would walk across a large, empty parking lot (a short cut) in bare feet with our rolled-up towels under our arms. Sometimes, we would race for we both loved to run. I remember the tiny stones that covered the pavement and having to watch out for broken glass. My hairbrush would sometimes fall out of my towel, and I had to run back and pick it up. We would stop at the water fountain for a drink before our swim. Dwayne would put his finger over the tap, which caused the water to spray up in the air to cool us off. In the first few summers after Dad was gone, I pretended to be a scuba diver in search for him. I had visions of him floating under the water as I swam. His stiff body would spin around and around ever so slowly. His eyes were closed, and he was dressed in black pants, a long black overcoat, and black-laced shoes. I had hoped to find a message in a bottle. "I'll send an SOS to the world…I hope that someone gets my message in a bottle…" (The Police, 1979). I never got that message in the bottle, as the water turned murky. I swam up to the ledge of the pool with my heart pounding as I caught my breath. *It was too late to save him!*

After our public swim was over, Dwayne and I would usually stop at a variety store and purchase a Lola, an ice treat which came in lemon, orange, cherry, or grape. I enjoyed the lemon while Dwayne's favourite was either grape or cherry (which seemed to describe the intensity of his inner being). Squeezing the sides of the papered triangle up and down created juices that would drip down to the bottom. Once the ice lost its colour, we swigged back the juice that floated at the bottom.

Water was a constant challenge for me after Dad was gone. It was now tainted and became my adversary. *Would an undercurrent take me down?* I fought back with hours of jumping, diving, cannonballing into the water at the community pool determined to win this battle. I could never avoid water—I enjoyed it so much. After a tough battle, I came to terms with it, and my discomfort around it started to fade. I made peace with water!

"Yellow Submarine" by the Beatles was a popular song and a play which our grade five class put on. The story was about a cheerful music-loving paradise under the sea called Pepperland. It was under attack by the Blue Meanies who hated music. An old sailor named Fred reactivates the yellow submarine and saves the band. A small group of us were sea creatures. I was a green sea turtle and others were fish dressed in orange, blue with black fins. Some of the boys were Blue Meanies. We all sang "We all live in a yellow submarine, yellow submarine, yellow submarine. Sky of blue and sea of green, every one of us have all we need." Our class made a large submarine out of cardboard and painted it bright yellow. In a make-believe way I wished Dad had fought off the Blue Meanies and was rescued by the yellow submarine.

My search for Dad continued in other places, as I hoped it was a terrible mistake of identity and that I would "see his face in a crowded place…" such as a shopping mall, amusement park or a movie theatre, and he would be back home. I prayed that the phone would ring, and it was him saying he would be home soon. Months turned into years, and I began to understand that Stevie Wonder's "Cherie Amour" lyrics "distant as the Milky Way" was how far away Dad was.

Enjoying a swim!

CHAPTER 8

Dreams

"Dream weaver, I believe you can get me through the night…oh Dream Weaver…I believe we can reach the morning light…" - Gary Wright, 1975

A dreamcatcher over my bed might have offered some comfort. Long white feathers with beads of teal blue could have had the power to slide good dreams upon me and trap the bad dreams in the web. The early morning light would banish those bad dreams away.

I had many dreams after Dad passed away, and there was always a disconnection in each one. I had visions of Dad's silhouette, but his face was blackened out or it would appear fuzzy. It reminded me of people being interviewed on *W5* who did not want to be identified for various reasons. Other times, I would only see his back or side profile from a long distance. I would try to communicate with him and ask questions like "What exactly happened?" He appeared mute or just not willing to talk to me. He was all around me but would just vanish, like Chantel Kreviazuk's song

"Surrounded": "…it's all around me, you surround me like a circle…you know I remember the bomb, and I still hear the bomb…." The bomb will always be walking home to the shattering news of Dad's death.

A notable dream I experienced one evening showed Dad's shadow by the waterfront. It was nighttime and he was pacing back and forth along the concrete pier and looking out toward the Toronto Skyline. Suddenly he stepped forward and tripped. He smashed his head against the icy concrete edge and tumbled into the freezing water. Appearing unconscious, he eventually sunk beneath the deep water. Quickly, my dream shifted to a police officer carrying a large brown envelope that had official documents in it. An embossed stamp was placed on the bottom of the paper with a scribbled signature (I could see through the transparent envelope). Quickly, I took out a magnifying glass that I typically used to view handwriting samples and read "bruising and contusions to the head and neck. A head injury that resulted in an unfortunate drowning." I woke with my heart racing with panic. I learned a bad fall or severe blow to the head can cause a vein to rupture between the skull and the brain's surface, which can be fatal. So, this dream brought a new possible cause of death. *A horrible accident!*

Recurring dreams of dark, stormy waters were common for me. The water seemed frothy with lots of white-capped waves. The place was *familiar,* as if I were around it before. It appeared to be at a dead-end road that opened to a larger body of water. There were lots of large rocks built up around the water, and the water splashed hard against the rocks. I was *terrified,* as I would wake up with my heart racing and trying to catch my breath.

I enjoyed watching a TV series called *The Night Stalker* that aired in the evenings in 1974-1975. It was about a newspaper reporter who investigated mysterious crimes that the police sometimes would not follow up on. After the show, I would turn in for the night and awaken with a nightmare, so our family doctor recommended that I stop watching the show.

I never dreamed about the real memories I had with Dad, such as him eating a huge plate of mashed potatoes, a three-dimensional square, step dancing, sitting in his truck, our vacations, and that special wink he would always give me in his rear-view mirror. But I guess those special memories were saved for daydreams, and nighttime was for troubling dreams.

Eventually, my dreams about Dad faded and were replaced with more current events in my life. Time was moving forward, and I was too.

CHAPTER 9

Moving On

1976-1984

In 1976, we moved into a large three-bedroom townhouse just twenty minutes northwest of our previous place. It was a necessary move for us all, as there were just too many memories of Dad at our old place.

I was starting grade seven at my fourth elementary school and blossoming into a teenager. We had lots of practice adapting to new situations. Mom was happy with our new place and especially liked all the extra space. Mom kept house, as she did not feel ready to be working. Supper was usually ready right after school, and on Fridays we often ordered a pizza or had fish and chips. We all took turns cleaning the supper dishes and sometimes traded off nights between each other as we had sporting events to attend, or other plans made. Sibling rivalry was a given and we had plenty. We fought over the rogers box quite often. Mom was always good about venturing off if we needed something for school whether it was school supplies or returning running shoes that did not fit. Jean overalls were the upcoming craze and hard to find due to their popularity, but I managed to find a pair in my size at a downtown store. Mom took the long trip by bus to the city and grabbed me the last pair. Keeping up with the latest trends was important to me and I was grateful for everything I received. She did the same for my siblings and we always received a birthday card with a bit of money to buy something special that we desired.

Mom started dating a man by the name of Edmond, who worked as a land surveyor and was from the east coast. He would drop by each week after work wearing a white tee, ridiculous white shorts, and work boots much like dad wore. Edmond would never replace Dad, but in an odd way we liked him right away. Whenever he removed his work boots at the front door, tiny little stones splattered all over our welcome mat. My siblings and I called him Ed-stone and would laugh uncontrollably when we thought about the name. He was a good sport and took it in stride. Ed-stone loved cartoons, especially *The Bugs Bunny/Road Runner Hour*. "On with the show, this is it!" Ed-stone brought humour to our home that was missing. It really was on the with show—on with our lives…this is it!

On summer weekends, Ed-stone took us all up to his cottage for some boating. We enjoyed this so much, as we missed going away on vacation. One afternoon while Ed-stone and Mom sat on the back deck, we all mischievously went into the spare room and snooped around. We opened some drawers and found a lot of *Playboy* magazines. In shock, we decided to throw them all over the living floor. We were still testing and getting to know Ed-stone. Mom was furious! Well, our weekend ended quickly, and Mom broke up with Ed-stone for a time. Mom was upset with us and thought we were trying to break them up by pulling that stunt. They started seeing each other again a month later, and he forgave us. Mom was not so happy with him anymore and would say he was cheap. She wanted gifts and to be taken out for dinner. Ed-stone believed it was waste of money to go out for dinner and appreciated home-cooked meals instead. The relationship ended sometime in the late summer of 1977. We missed Ed-stone, as he had really grown on us.

I started my first year of high school in the fall of 1977, and I was excited about the new change. I wore my fashionable earth shoes and some boo-boo jeans that were Levi's with slight flaws but great prices. The parties were starting, and the music was loud. We "gonna rock it up, roll it up, do it all, have a ball, Saturday night…." by Bay City Rollers—S-A-T-U-R-D-A-Y night! I wore a plaid shirt, as the Bay City Rollers wore plaid. My black army shirt was another fashionable item at the time. I enjoyed walking through the halls during period changes, as it was a time to check everybody out and get to know people. We had a huge juke box in the cafeteria and music like Supertramp with "So, give a little bit, give a little bit of your love to me" and Toto singing "Hold the line, love isn't always on time…" serenaded us and our peanut butter sandwiches or the fries with gravy we typically bought on a Friday. The adolescent hormones were running wild, as we all rocked to the lyrics of love.

My first year went well, and I was progressing toward grade ten. Dwayne followed next and decided to go to the Catholic high school nearby. Janice was in grade eight and Ben in grade seven. Mom and Janice were arguing a lot and just seemed to clash. Janice's best friend had moved away, and she was really having trouble finding new friends. I know now, the alert button should have been placed on Janice, long before this time, as red flags were evident that she needed professional intervention to help support her through the stages of development (school age/ adolescence and early adulthood).

Our home environment could be quite tense at times. It made for a difficult night if mom were upset as she would openly express what a heavy burden she was left to deal with. It was not easy for us to hear, as we were grieving too. Mom was going through her own private turmoil. Other times Mom would seem better, which made for a more stable evening. During this time, we had a few family counselling sessions, but not enough to improve things. Ben attended the Big Brothers program for a period of time as well.

In the fall of 1979, Aunt Lorrie offered to take Janice into her home and have her attend high school in Mississauga. Mom agreed and Janice happily went. She was successful in her first year of high school and had a boyfriend. She worked part-time at the local variety store. Unfortunately, Aunt Lorrie was upset with my mom always phoning and interfering with how she raised Janice. My sister was stuck in the middle of it all and played both sides of authority, which caused a lot of upset for everyone. Aunt Lorrie phoned Mom one evening and told her it was not going to work and that she would only let Janice stay if she could legally adopt her. Mom was not sure what to do but decided she would not allow it. Another idea was to put Janice in foster care before her sixteenth birthday, as she could do what she wanted once she turned sixteen. A family offered to take her, and they happened to have a salon in their basement where Janice could have learned hairstyling. Janice visited but did not want to live there, so Mom was left not knowing what to do again.

Janice then moved into her boyfriend's home, but that situation was short-lived as well because her boyfriend's mother found it stressful and complained that Janice was not doing anything productive.

Around that time, I found an upper-floor apartment in a house for Jan and gave her first and last months' rent. She had enrolled in an apprenticeship program to train as a hairstylist instead of returning to high school. The government assisted her with financial help to pay rent and living expenses. This was a wonderful opportunity, and I was happy for Jan. Disappointingly, Jan never followed through with the entire program. She had my support; however, it came with boundaries. I was not in position to be her caregiver or guardian (parent) that she so desperately needed. It was an extremely difficult time for me and I hated that I was having to be confronted with such a dilemma. Jan had to accept the reality that she was pretty much on her own; she had to get it together somehow and find away to take responsibility for her actions and choices. That was the reality for all of us due to our lack of parental guidance. Our home was falling apart at the seams. The age of sixteen was the age of fending for yourself. "This is the end of the innocence," Don Henley sang.

Things went terribly wrong for Jan after that! Mom should have reconsidered Aunt Lorrie's offer or foster care. Janice needed structure and rules, as she was not ready to take on the world. Leaving the school system during those formative years and not partaking in skills training or even working much was damaging for an already at-risk child. Janice continued to demonstrate complete irresponsibility and a disregard for societal rules. Then she began to hang out with the wrong people and made very poor choices.

I briefly stayed at my boyfriend's house before I rented a very small room and found a job as a receptionist. I completed my last couple of years of high school through correspondence. My weekends were spent hanging out with my good friends listening to the music, as the Doobie Brothers sang "whoa oh whoa…listen to the music." Shuffling cards, smoking Du Maurier (red pack) and drinking beer gave us a feeling of pleasure despite any issues we were dealing with. I started visiting Mom every other week; it worked better that way. Dwayne and Ben were still at home. Janice was running wild somewhere and nowhere in particular.

Eventually, I rented a two-bedroom apartment with shared accommodations which provided a better living arrangement. My various office jobs bored me to death, as I would move on after about a year for a new experience. "My job is very boring, I'm an office clerk…The only thing that helps me pass the time away, is knowing I'll be back at Echo Beach some day." Martha and the Muffins international single hit filled me with anticipation of good things to come. My Echo Beach was weekends, and it did not matter if there was sand or water—it was beach enough for me! MTV launched in the 1980s, which made it possible to watch music videos around the clock. "Video Killed the Radio Star" by Buggles was our introduction to this emerging time.

1984-2001

Around 1984, Ben was experiencing increased anxiety trying to deal with home life and the changes that adolescents go through. He was referred to an amazing therapist and it was highly recommended that he should not return home.

Co-op housing that supports adolescents transitioning into adulthood was organized for Ben. Ben was receptive to the suggestions and cooperated fully. He successfully finished his grade twelve and then started working at various jobs to support himself. He was eventually diagnosed with obsessive-compulsive disorder (OCD) and began taking medication to help even things out. Ben mentioned that his weekly talks with his therapist kept him strong and resilient. As well sessions with Dr. S (CAMH) filled him with hope and faith in recovery.

Dwayne was the only one who continued to live with Mom for just a little bit longer, ultimately supporting himself at nineteen. Mom had a soft spot for him…I would say he was her favourite. He was also diagnosed with OCD a few years later. My brothers kept in touch and would hang out sometimes, however, their temperaments were quite different and eventually there were longer spaces between their visits.

My boyfriend and I managed to rent an affordable one-bedroom apartment not far away from where we worked. I continued doing clerical work and started my college education part-time. 1985 arrived, and my high school sweetheart got down on one knee to ask me to marry him. The answer was *YES!* We planned the wedding for later that year.

It was an exciting year all around! Bob Geldof (The Boomtown Rats) and Midge Ure (Ultravox) spearheaded Live Aid, a concert to raise millions of dollars for famine relief that affected Ethiopia, in July. We cranked the TV up loud as we watched U2, Phil Collins, Dire Straits, Madonna, Bryan Adams and many more rock it out at Wembley Stadium. Queen blasted "Bohemian Rhapsody," "We Will Rock You" and "We Are the Champions" among many other hits, and Freddie Mercury entranced the audience with a powerful performance for the ages. "Ay-oh! Ay-oh!" he teasingly sang, and the crowd echoed him. "And we'll keep on fighting till the end…" If there had been a roof on the stadium that day, it would have been blown open by Queen's incredible performance.

It was snowing ever so beautifully, much like a snow globe you see at Christmas time, on the afternoon of our wedding in late November. Immediate family and a small group of friends attended our wedding ceremony. Dwayne, dressed in a black suit, walked me up to the altar of St. James Church. I wore a white wedding dress with a high-collared neckline designed for a winter wedding. We had a small gathering afterwards at my husband's family home and started our lives together with hopes of a wonderful future ahead.

By the spring of 1986, Janice was pressuring us to let her move in to our place. Having the three of us living together was simply not going to work considering Jan's complex needs and our living arrangement. We wanted our privacy just like any young couple, and the extra stress we would have to tolerate seemed too much to handle at that time. It felt like a *Sophie's Choice* moment (80s movie). Sophie's choice was between two children, my choice—of a different magnitude—was between two people I loved so much. My husband and I ended up leaving our apartment and moving away for a while. I wished I could have been better able to support Jan and protect her from an unfortunate outcome.

Janice was hospitalized the following year, which resulted in a long-term stay under psychiatric care to help her become a more responsible adult. She was diagnosed with a severe personality disorder, which is the most difficult to treat. It is only through time as the person ages that symptoms might decrease. I learned that they get tired and do not have the energy for all the disruption and drama they cause to themselves and others. Jan was put on all kinds of different medications trying to find the right one. During her hospitalization, my husband and I made regular visits, and sometimes I would travel on my own to see her. We would go for long walks, hang out at the park, and end our visit with words of encouragement. Janice was eventually released, placed in supportive housing, and given outpatient community support. We visited a few times, but I was informed (and I recognized) she was further complicating her illness with continued use of additional substances that were harmful to her condition. At that point, my decision was to distance myself.

Around that time, Dwayne and Ben found blue-collar jobs. I continued my boring office jobs and eagerly waited for Fridays, as the office closed at noon. I remember "Livin' on a Prayer" by Bon Jovi piercing out of a random car while I took my forty-five-minute bus ride home one night. "We gotta hold on to what we got...we've got each other...and that's a lot..." We were holding on to our jobs, our apartment and each other. *We were all giving it our best shot!*

We enjoyed our concerts such as Genesis, Bruce Springsteen, Jeff Healy and Prism to name a few. One night my husband and I went for a drive and stopped at a hole-in-the-wall roadhouse that, to our surprise, had Trooper playing live. The venue was small, so the music was loud. I remember "Round, Round We Go"— "Round, round we go, round, round we go...you're turning me upside down."

and "Two for the Show" amongst other popular hits. Life was spinning round and round, and we were on the move. *A change in the weather!*

We bought our first home in early 1990 outside of the city. It was an adjustment for me living outside the city in a neighbourhood that was mostly full of young families. I was not even sure I wanted to stay, but I am glad I did. Eventually, we were blessed with the precious gift of two beautiful daughters! Life could not have been any better! Those early years were so special, as I loved spending the time at home with my girls. I never wanted to leave them with anyone, so it was difficult when I occasionally had to go to work. My husband would make things easier by folding laundry or emptying the dishwasher, which enabled me to rest or give more of my time to the girls. There was an overall feeling of contentment in our home with plenty of music to dance and circle around the kitchen in.

However, around late 2000 into 2001, I started to feel blue. It was not just a day or two, it started to last longer. I recognized that I stayed home too long, and it would have been a better idea to have gone back to work, especially around 2000 when the symptoms first emerged. I was not sleeping well, and eventually my appetite started to decrease. I felt a sense of hopelessness and had a difficult time doing any household tasks. In desperation, I went to see a counsellor, as it was a benefit I could access as a student enrolled in an online university course. He believed I was in a situational depression because I was torn between being a stay-home mother and a working mother. I recognized I was very fortunate to have had the choice to be at home, although it came with some financial sacrifice too. It was a huge dilemma and no doubt influenced by a difficult family history. I wanted to wait until both my girls were in school full-time, but clearly it was too long of a wait.

My counsellor recommended reading *You Can Be Happy No Matter What* by Richard Carlson Ph.D. It discusses five principles for keeping life in perspective: our thoughts, moods, separate realities, feelings, and the present moment. My family doctor suggested an anti-depressant to help me get through this *situational* depression. I reluctantly filled the prescription, but it sat in my cupboard for a couple of weeks. I was hesitating because I saw what the medications had done to Janice. I was *afraid!* However, after another few weeks it was necessary that I start taking the medication or the situation was going to get worse. Slowly, week by week, I started to feel a little better and was able to finish Dr. Carlson's (psychotherapist) book. This book became very special to me when I needed a reminder of how to put life into perspective. Six weeks after starting the medication, I was smiling and felt motivated regardless of it being a temporary solution; I started feeling better and was lucky not to have experienced any side effects. A new appreciation for the beauty of trees and flowers was suddenly embraced. The biggest improvement was not feeling stuck anymore and wanting to do things. I saw light at the end of the tunnel, and I knew everything would be just fine. I found full-time employment within the education field that gave me summers off with my family. My girls were going to before- and after-school care, and I was okay with that now. *I had my life back!*

CHAPTER 10

Funeral 2

It was summer 2002, Dwayne and I arranged to meet at the mall for lunch. We were not carrying phones or texting at that time. Unfortunately, after circling around the mall over and over, we were unable find each other. Frustrated and disappointed, I decided to go home. We spoke later that evening and decided to reschedule after my vacation was over. The last thing I said to Dwayne was "Take it easy." I realized he was having difficulty and had just moved into his own apartment. He had another upcoming knee surgery and was experiencing a lot of pain.

My husband and I were taking our two daughters up north for a week at a cottage resort near Algonquin Park. We loved the fact that we could sit on the veranda, see Oxtongue Lake, and watch our girls closely as they swam and jumped on a water trampoline with all the other children in the area. There was a big playground with a sandy beach that offered the kids hours of fun, and the resort organized a scavenger hunt for all the children near the end of the week. My husband and I played horseshoes, basketball and took the girls on hikes nearby. I was feeling like myself again thanks to the medication I initially refused. Our evenings sometimes ended with roasting marshmallows or making smores around the fire. I remember the racoons being exceptionally friendly one evening. They were looking for sweet snacks too!

We arrived home just before noon on Sunday, July 7, after a wonderful holiday! Shortly after that I received a call from my mom, who was in hysterics. She told me Dwayne was *DEAD.* My heart sank as I sat on the couch, listening. She had trouble speaking and gave me only a little information before the call ended abruptly. Shock ran through my body. My husband walked in the living room, and I said, "It was my mom and it's not good…Dwayne has died."

I can only remember hours of not being able to get off the couch. I did not want to be consoled. In fact, I just wanted to be left alone; *numb with news.* My reaction was much like when I got the news of Dad's passing: *frozen.* Flashbacks streamed through my head like an old film reel running through a little projector. Dwayne and I racing through the parking lot to get to the pool, riding our bikes, playing One-Man Chase and him walking on crutches as he was healing from another knee surgery. It went on and on. The film strip began to tangle all around me. The memory of our last phone call and the shocking reality that we would not see each other again was tough to take.

My husband took the girls to the park for a while, as I had a few telephone calls coming my way. At supper time I told the girls about the passing of their uncle in a gentle way and explained he had not been feeling well for a long time. I spared them some details, and eventually shared more as they got older. It was just like Mom sparing us some details. My girls were nine and six years old, around the same ages as my brothers and sister when we got the news of our father passing so many years prior. This time it was me breaking the news, not the priest. Uncle Dwayne had a few visits with the girls over the years and was always so happy to see them. My oldest daughter wrote a poem about Uncle Dwayne, and my youngest daughter processed in her own little way; *quietly.*

Ben and I have always shared a sixth sense or intuition about Dwayne, and we both previously had numerous dreams that Dwayne was dead, dying or in an awful troublesome situation. We knew of Dwayne's struggles and challenges, but I was surprised to hear how out of control it had gotten. He was dealing with obsessive-compulsive disorder as well as addiction to alcohol and eventually Percocet that was prescribed for his knee. Dwayne's pelvis and right knee were broken after being hit by a car crossing a highway years before. A few knee surgeries followed afterwards, which were painful, and Percocet was prescribed to manage the pain. Dwayne had carried a lot of anger and sadness over the loss of our father, and he struggled with it. He was quiet, kind, and generous by nature. He was reluctant to listen to advice and did not appreciate anyone telling him what to do. I found it difficult to connect with him most of the time. At the time of his death, Dwayne was not in a relationship. His two sons from a past relationship were just eleven and seven years old. He adored his boys and spoke lovingly about them to me. He especially enjoyed throwing the football back and forth with his boys.

Dwayne's voicemail was full, and people had been trying to get a hold of him for over a week. Neighbours were complaining about an odour in the hallway for about five days. Police were finally called, and they opened my brother's apartment door. Dwayne's remains were found on his couch. An autopsy was not performed due to the circumstances, but the police suspect he died from an accidental or intentional overdose of Percocet and alcohol that caused his breathing to slow down and heart to stop.

I do know that nine months prior Dwayne was at a dance hall where he went into distress and became unconscious. The paramedics arrived and got Dwayne to the hospital in time. Mom mentioned that the doctor told Dwayne "We just about lost you." He was warned about the pain medication and the consequences of mixing alcohol with it, but his ability to make wise decisions and use sound judgement had fallen to the wayside. He was caught up in a foggy false reality of *addiction*. Accidental or deliberate? There is room for debate. I had a lot of different emotions to sort through. Eventually, I got to the place of holding no ill feeling towards Dwayne, just *sadness*. His boys would have to carry on with out him. It was history repeating itself.

My husband went to pick up Dwayne's clothes and other personal belongings from his apartment. I was unable to go and wanted to be alone with my sorrow, just like the morning of Dad's church funeral many years earlier. Later in the day, my kitchen was filled with boxes of Dwayne's clothes, possessions, and the smell of death. *Final and ghostly!* As I sat in the kitchen grief-stricken, I had to help plan a funeral.

We had to arrange a memorial service and a burial quickly for our brother Dwayne. We held the service at Mount Pleasant Cemetery, which offered a charming chapel for memorial services. A beautifully landscaped garden surrounded the chapel, and a very tall weeping willow provided shade from the hot sun. People started arriving and sat outside the chapel on garden benches surrounding a garden pond. Mass began at 1:00 p.m. The chapel was full, and family and friends placed many pictures of Dwayne around the front altar. Our family took our seats in the front pew, and the minister began with a prayer. Ben spoke about Dwayne's love of hockey, baseball and them spending time together throwing the football around. I talked about our gift of running and enjoyment of swimming that we shared. Ben and I focused on the positive times we shared with Dwayne. We all prayed and had moments of silence. "Amazing Grace" was played on the organ, and the lyrics "I once was lost and now I'm found…" pierced the chapel. More silence than prayer followed.

The memorial for Dwayne ended with the song "Now You're Gone" by his favourite band, Whitesnake. The lyrics "But now you're gone, there's an emptiness closing around me…" caught the air as the chapel emptied and condolences were exchanged. Ben and Tina, new parents to a baby girl, offered up the event room located at their condominium for a gathering of close friends and family to honour Dwayne's life. We shared memories and supported each other as best we could. The evening ended early.

Dwayne was cremated and buried with his father. We all know that would have been Dwayne's wish.

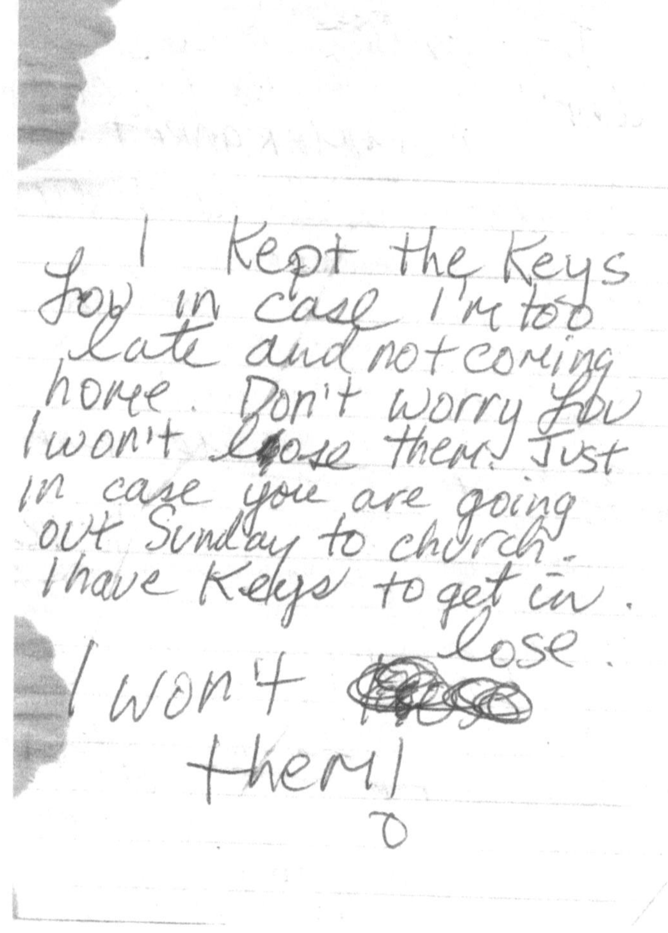

Dwayne's Handwriting Sample 1

Dwayne's writing sample reveals a slant that indicates a mild to moderate emotional responsiveness. He could be highly responsive depending on the situation. Dwayne put pressure on the pen indicating a deep emotional nature as he carried past hurts with intensity. Lack of approach strokes and flourishes indicate frankness. He would quickly get to the point in a conversation and express his opinion regardless of outcome. Defiance popped up in his *k*. He was not afraid of challenge or opposition.

He suffered with pain in his nee,
I should have made him some tea.

I will always miss him,
I bet he was kind of slim.

I feel very sorry for his boys,
But they will always remember his toys.

My mom said he was tender hearted,
I wish this death never started.

He liked sports very much,
But now he won't be able to touch.

He will always look down from Heven,
and see his boys who are eleven and seven.

In Heven he will be very glad
to see once again, his dad.

My Oldest Daughter's Poem for Uncle Dwayne

CHAPTER 11

"Knowing"

"I can see clearly now the rain is gone; I can see all obstacles in my way…It's going to be a bright sunshiny day. Look straight ahead, there's nothing but blue skies."

- Jimmy Cliff

I continue to live my life with the mystery of what might have transpired between my last moment with Dad at the staircase and the time leading up to his death. Was he alone somewhere contemplating his departure from this world? The battery of his car was taken from his vehicle. Was it stolen or was it used as a heavy object to weigh him down into the depths of the water? When I think about the dream of Dad falling on the icy pier resulting in a head injury and unfortunate drowning, I know it would have been easier to deal with and understand; the lesser of two evils. In 1999, I requested a copy of the coroner's report and read through it very carefully. It stated that there were no signs of trauma. Although it appears he decided to end his life, I have always left a little room for doubt that maybe it was a horrible accident.

Getting the news of Dwayne's death in 2002 felt very unfair, but who says life is fair? The coincidence of Dwayne and Dad both subtracted from our lives at thirty-eight years old was shockingly hard to endure. The circumstances around their deaths like the freezing cold temperatures that Dad succumbed to and the extreme heatwave that Dwayne's last hours encompassed were strangely clashing. They both struggled with mental health and addiction that lead to their untimely departures. Was Dwayne's death accidental or deliberate? Both deaths have some room for uncertainty. The wallets they left behind were filled with identification, phone numbers and medical appointment cards that traced their last steps on Earth and have been laid to rest in a memory box.

Mom passed away of dementia in the summer of 2016 just before her eightieth birthday. She had been in a nursing home and had given up on life. She mostly slept. She started refusing to eat and take medication. My visits were short near the end, as she wanted to be alone. Mom died alone! She was cremated and buried with her second husband, as she requested. After speaking with her family doctor, I found out she had been diagnosed with bipolar disorder in the 1980s. Clearly, Mom struggled, and parenting was extremely challenging for her. The teenage years were turbulent and Mom didn't know how to deal with it or want the full responsibility anymore. Mom wanted to move on with her own life while still having connections with us. It was almost like she was pushing a fast forward button and wanting to be an "empty nester" sooner than real time allowed. She showed love in ways, yet she was reluctant or unable to share the good stories that we needed to hear about Dad. Sharing photographs of him and his children together would have reassured us of the love we shared. It would have helped us with the healing process.

These family tragedies were obstacles that were in my way, but they did not defeat me. I am one of many people out there that has had to deal with incredible loss, so I keep my life in perspective. My experiences could have made me bitter, but I was humbled instead. Growing up as an adult child was obviously not a role I would have wished for, but my inner child was somehow protected. Some people call it being "young-hearted."

As an early childhood educator and child and youth worker, I know that the brain is not fully developed until the age of twenty-one. Traumatic childhoods cause changes in the areas of the brain that deal with stress. The brain is rewired differently after childhood trauma. Genetics, temperament, and environment play an important role in how resilient we become.

Witnessing firsthand the downside of what can happen to people who are institutionalized, over medicated, and even misdiagnosed, not to mention street drugs to further complicate a diagnosis, resulted in me becoming extremely vigilant around the mental health system. Although safeguarded and controlled, I have observed the sparkle in people's eyes replaced with a dull glaze. Medication is a double-edged sword for some people. Some would say they fall between the cracks.

Lastly, I acknowledge there are successful outcomes for a lot of people dealing with mental health and addiction while navigating through these doors. I applaud and look forward to continuous advancement and initiatives from both the

Centre for Addiction and Mental Health (CAMH) and Bell Let's Talk to help reduce the stigma around mental health and addiction to build better tomorrows for people dealing with these issues.

Reflection Letters

Dear Dad:

As children, we grew up hearing different stories about what might have happened to you. This troubled us all. The sense of despair and the inability to understand the consequences of your actions were eventually realized as I became an adult; if that is in fact what happened. Still there are questions that will never be answered. You tried hard to make amends with mom, but it seemed impossible, as well, dealing with a significant job loss that took its toll. No matter what, I am grateful for the memories that I do have of you!

P.S. I remember the pup you delivered to our door when living near the CNE. Animals really do bring joy to a family, especially in a time of difficulty. In 2003, my family welcomed "Pearle" a Bichon Frise in a fluffy white jacket; the size of a kleenex box to bless our home.

Love always, Shelline

Dear Mom:

Thanks for visiting my family on those special Sundays! I will always remember our dinners at Swiss Chalet. You tried your best and I will always love you!

Ben xo

P.S. Dad, I never knew you. You left too early. Why?... Dwayne, you are thought of often and I enjoy the connection I have with your son Jimmy and his family.

Dear Reader:

We all have personal stories that contain the details of our journey through life, and some of us will experience more misfortune that others. I hope my story inspires others to keep pushing through and know that you are going to see better days ahead.

S. Kovacs

65

Ben and I remain close today!

Enjoy the music!!

MY PLAYLIST!

Bud the Spud – Stompin' Tom Connors

My Cherie Amour – Stevie Wonder

Stompin' Grounds – Stompin' Tom Connors

Manteca & On the Sunny Side of the Street – Dizzy Gillespie

American Pie – Don McLean

Night Search (*Jaws* Soundtrack) by John Williams

Great White Shark Chase & Shark Attack – (*Jaws* Soundtrack) by John Williams

A Whiter Shade of Pale – Procol Harum

Sound Explosion (1973) album

Doo Wah Diddy Diddy – Manfred Mann

Mother's Little Helper – The Rolling Stones

Loco-motion – Little Eva

The Country Waltz – Don Messer & His Islanders

Harper Valley P.T.A. – Jeannie C. Riley

Raindrops Keep Fallin' on My Head – B.J. Thomas

Message in a Bottle – The Police

Yellow Submarine – The Beatles

Dream Weaver – Gary Wright

Surrounded – Chantal Kreviazuk

The Bugs Bunny/Road Runner Hour Theme

Saturday Night – Bay City Rollers

Give a Little Bit – Supertramp

Hold the Line – Toto

The End of the Innocence – Don Henley

Listen to the Music – Dobbie Brothers

Echo Beach – Martha and the Muffins

Video Killed the Radio Star – Buggles

We Will Rock You – Queen

Sophie's Choice Love Theme – Marvin Hamlisch

Livin' on a Prayer – Bon Jovi

Hysteria – Def Leppard

Round, Round We Go – Trooper

Amazing Grace – Piano Instrumental, YouTube

Now You're Gone – Whitesnake

I Can See Clearly Now – Jimmy Cliff

Nature CD – Sounds of the Ocean

Music- Art Project- 2008
(by My Youngest Daughter) - Def Leppard

Enjoying Nature!